Silas Weir Mitchell

A Psalm of Deaths and Other Poems

Silas Weir Mitchell

A Psalm of Deaths and Other Poems

ISBN/EAN: 9783744781541

Printed in Europe, USA, Canada, Australia, Japan

Cover: Foto ©Thomas Meinert / pixelio.de

More available books at **www.hansebooks.com**

A PSALM OF DEATHS
AND OTHER POEMS

S. WEIR MITCHELL M. D. LL. D. Harv.

AUTHOR OF "THE HILL OF STONES AND OTHER POEMS" "A MASQUE
AND OTHER POEMS" "THE CUP OF YOUTH" ETC

BOSTON AND NEW YORK
HOUGHTON, MIFFLIN AND COMPANY
The Riverside Press, Cambridge
1890

The Riverside Press, Cambridge, Mass., U. S. A.
Printed by H. O. Houghton & Company.

To

JAMES RUSSELL LOWELL

CONTENTS.

———◆———

A PSALM OF DEATHS.

A PSALM OF DEATHS.

———◆———

OF ONE WHO FELL ON THE WAY.

'T is but one more to-morrow. Thou art gray
With many a death of many a yesterday.
O yearning heart that lacked the athlete's force
And, stumbling, fell upon the beaten course,
And looked, and saw with ever glazing eyes
Some lower soul that seemed to win the prize!
Lo, Death, the just, who comes to all alike,
Life's sorry scales of right anew shall strike.
Forth, through the night, on unknown shores to win
The peace of God unstirred by sense of sin!
There love without desire shall, like a mist
At evening precious to the drooping flower,
Possess thy soul in ownership, and kissed
By viewless lips, whose touch shall be a dower
Of genius and of winged serenity,
Thou shalt abide in realms of poesy.
There soul hath touch of soul, and there the great
Cast wide to welcome thee joy's golden gate.

Free born to thoughts that ever age on age
Caressed sweet singers in their sacred sleep,
Thy soul shall enter on its heritage
Of God's unuttered wisdom. Thou shalt sweep
With hand assured the ringing lyre of life,
Till the fierce anguish of its bitter strife,
Its pain, death, discord, sorrow, and despair,
Break into rhythmic music. Thou shalt share
The prophet-joy that kept forever glad
God's poet-souls when all a world was sad.
Enter and live ! Thou hast not lived before ;
We are but soul-cast shadows. Ah, no more
The heart shall bear the burdens of the brain ;
Now shall the strong heart think, nor think in vain.
In the dear company of peace, and those
Who bore for man life's utmost agony,
Thy soul shall climb to cliffs of still repose,
And see before thee lie Time's mystery,
And that which is God's time, Eternity ;
Whence sweeping over thee dim myriad things,
The awful centuries yet to be, in hosts
That stir the vast of heaven with formless wings,
Shall cast for thee their shrouds, and, like to ghosts,
Unriddle all the past, till awed and still
Thy soul the secret hath of good and ill.
   1889.

OF THOSE REMEMBERED.

THERE is no moment when our dead lose power ;
Unsignaled, unannounced they visit us.
Who calleth them I know not. Sorrowful,
They haunt reproachfully some venal hour
In days of joy, and when the world is near,
And for a moment scourge with memories
The money changers of the temple-soul.
In the dim space between two gulfs of sleep,
Or in the stillness of the lonely shore,
They rise for balm or torment, sweet or sad,
And most are mine where, in the kindly woods,
Beside the child-like joy of summer streams,
The stately sweetness of the pine hath power
To call their kindred comforting anew.
Use well thy dead.   They come to ask of thee
What thou hast done with all this buried love,
The seed of purer life ?   Or has it fallen unused
In stony ways and brought thy life no gain ?
Wilt thou with gladness in another world
Say it has grown to forms of duty done
And ruled thee with a conscience not thine own ?
Another world !   How shall we find our dead ?

What forceful law shall bring us face to face?
Another world! What yearnings there shall guide?
Will love souls twinned of love bring near again?
And that one common bond of duty held
This living and that dead, when life was theirs?
Or shall some stronger soul, in life revered,
Bring both to touch, with nature's certainty,
As the pure crystal atoms of its kind
Draws into fellowship of loveliness?
   1889.

OF ONE DEAD.

THERE is a heart I knew in other days,
Not ever far from any one day's thought ;
One pure as are the purest. All the years
Of battle, or of peace, of joy or grief,
Take him no further from me. Oftentimes,
When the sweet honesty of some glad girl
Troubles my eyes, full suddenly I know
It is because one memory ever dear
Is matched a moment with its living kin.
Or when at hearing of some gallant deed
My throat fills, and I may not dare to say
The quick praise in me, then I know, alas !
'T is by this dear dead nobleness my soul is stirred.
He lived, he loved, he died. Small epitaph !
What hour of duty in the long grim wards
Poisoned his life, I know not. Painfully
He sickened, yearning for the strife of War
That went its thunderous way unhelped of him ;
And then he died. A little duty done ;
A little love for many, much for me,
And that was all beneath this earthly sun.
    1889.

PAINED UNTO DEATH.

ONE life I knew was a psalm, a terrible psalm of pain,
Dark with disaster of torment, heart and brain
Racked as if God were not, and hope a dream
Some demon memory brought to bid blaspheme
All life's dismembered sweetness.　" Peace, be still,"
I hear her spirit whisper.　" His the will
That from some unseen bow of purpose sped
This sorrow of my torture."　God of dread !
The long sad years that justify the dead,
The long sad years at last interpreted :
Serene as clouds that over stormy seas,
At sunset rise with mystery of increase,
One with the passionate deep that gave them birth
Her gentled spirit rose on wings of peace,
And was and was not of this under earth.
　1890.

THE WHOLE CREATION GROANETH.

ART glad with the gladness of youth in thy veins,
In thy hands, for the spending, earth's joy and its
    gains ?
Lo ! winged with storm shadows the torturers come,
And to-night, or to-morrow, thy lips shall be dumb,
Thy hands wet with pain-thrills, thy nerves, that were
    strung
To fineness of sense by earth's pleasure, be wrung
With pangs the beast knows not, nor he who in tents
Lives lone in the desert, and knoweth not whence
The bread of the morrow. Pain like to a mist
Goeth up from the earth, and is lost, and none wist
Why ever it cometh, why ever it waits
In the heart of our loves, like a foe in our gates.
Lo! summer and sunshine are over the land, —
Who marshaled yon billows? what wind of command
Drives ever their merciless march on the strand?
Thus, dateless, relentless, the children of strife
None have seen, on the sun-lighted beaches of life
March ever the ravening billows of pain.
O heart that is breaking go ask of the brain
If aught God hath spent is but squandered in vain ?

Yea, where is the sunshine of centuries dead?
Yea, where are the raindrops of yesterday shed?
God findeth anew his lost light in the force
That holdeth the world on its resolute course,
And surely, as surely the madness of pain
Shall pass into wisdom, and come back again
An angel of courage if thou art the one
That knoweth to deal with the lightnings that stun
To blindness the many.   A thousand shall fall
By the waysides of life, and in helplessness call
For the death-alms which nature gives freely to all;
And one, like the jewel, shall break the fierce light
That seareth thine eyeballs, and cast through the night
The colours that read us its meaning aright.
   1890.

IN THE VALLEY OF THE SHADOW.

THE CENTURION.

A dark cell of the Circus Maximus. The Centurion and his child.

"FATHER! keep me ; hold me closer.   Are they lions
    that I hear ?
Once beside the Syrian desert where we camped I
    heard them near
While our servants made us music; and there 's music
    now.   'T was night,
And 't is very dark here, father.   There we had the
    stars for light.
Father, father! that was laughter, and the noise of
    many hands.
Why is it they make so merry ?   Shall we laugh soon ?
    On the sands
How you smiled to see my terror.   'What,' you said,
    'A Roman maid
Tremble in the Legion's camp!   A Roman maiden
    and afraid ! '

"Hush! Who called ? Who called me ? Mother! Surely
    that was mother's voice."

But the gray centurion trembling murmured, " Little
    one, rejoice ! "
Yet a single moan of sorrow broke the guard his man-
    hood set,
While the sweetness of her forehead with a storm of
    tears was wet.
And he answered, as she questioned, " That was but
    the rain God sends
To the flowers he loves," — then lower, — " Grief and
    I are friends."

"Father, father, now 't is quiet.   Was it mother? I am
    cold.
Who, I wonder, feeds my carp? who, I wonder, at the
    fold
Combs my lambs? who prunes my roses? Think you
    they will keep us long
From the sunshine? Hark, the lions! Ah! they must
    be fierce and strong ! "

" Peace, my daughter.   Soon together we shall walk
    through gardens fair,
Where the lilies psalms are singing, and the roses
    whisper prayer."
" Who will bring us to the garden ? "   " Christ ! Thou
    wilt not hear him call ;
Suddenly wide doors shall open ; on thy eyes the sun
    shall fall ;
Thou shalt see God's lions, waiting, and, above, a liv-
    ing wall,

Yea, ten thousand faces waiting, come to help our holi-
day,
Music, flowers, and the Cæsar. — Rest upon my shoulder, lay
One small hand in mine, — and peace. A moment I
would think and pray.

"I am sore with shame and scourging, I, a Roman! I,
a knight!
Yea, if nobly born, the nobler for the birth of higher
light.
Was it pain, and was it shame? The lictor's rods fell
on a man;
On the God-man fell those scourges, and the bitter
drops that ran
Flowed from eyes that wept for millions, came of pain
none else can know,
An eternity of anguish, counted as the blood drops
flow.
Mine is but an atom's torment; mine shall bring eter-
nal gain;
His, the murder pangs of ages, paid with usury of pain.
Art thou weary of the darkness? Art thou cold, my
little maid?
Hast thou sorrow of my sorrow? Kiss my cheek. Be
not dismayed.
Lo, the nearness of one moment setteth age to lonely
thought,
Would his will but make us one ere yet his perfect will
be wrought.

That may not be.   Once, once only Love must drop
    the hand of love."
"Father, father! Hark, the lions!"   "Peace, my little
    one, my love,
Soon thy darkened cage will open, soon the voice of
    Christ will say,
'Come and be among my lilies, where the golden
    fountains play,
And an angel legion watches, and forever it is day.'
So, my hand upon thy shoulder.   You, so little! I, so
    tall!
Now, one kiss — earth's last! My darling."   Back the
    iron gate bolts fall.
Lo, the gray arena's quiet, and the faces waiting all,
Waiting, and the lions waiting, while the gray centu-
    rion smiled,
As, beneath the white velarium, fell God's sunlight on
    the child:
For a gentle voice above them murmured, "Forth, and
    have no fear,"
And the little maiden answered, "Lo, Christ Jesu, I
    am here!"
    1890.

A CANTICLE OF TIME.

Hours of grieving,
Hours of thought ;
Hours of believing,
Hours of naught.
Hours when the thieving
Fingers of doubt steal
Heart riches, faith bought.
Hours of spirit dearth,
Earthy, and born of earth,
When the racked universe
Is as a hell, or worse.
Hours when the curtain furled
Backward, revealed to us
Sorrowful sin gulfs,
Self had concealed from us.
Hours of wretchedness ;
Palsies that blind.
Hours none else can guess,
When the dumb mind
Faints, and heart wisdom
Is all that we find.
Hours when the cloud

That hides the unknown
A cumbering shroud
About us is thrown.
Hours that seem to part
Goodness and God.
Hours of fierce yearning,
When fruit of love's earning
Is shred from the heart.
Hours when no angel
Hovers o'er life.
Hours when no Christ-God
Pities our strife.
Yea, such is life !

Slowly the hours
Gather to years ;
They deal with our tears
That grief be not vain,
Gently as flowers
Deal with the rain.
Slowly the hours
Gather to years,
Sowing with roses
The graves of our fears.
Lo ! the dark crosses
Of torture's completeness
Mistily fade into
Symbols of sweetness,
And behold it is evening.

Swift through the grass
Shuttles of shadow
Silently pass,
Weaving at last
Tapestries sombre,
Solemn and vast,
And behold it is night!
Silence profound,
Solitude vacant
Of touch and of sound
Thy being doth bound.
This is death's loneliness,
Answerless, pitiless!
What of thee was king,
Let it crownless descend
From its tottering throne ;
Lo ! thou art alone,
And behold, 't is the end !

What sayeth the soul ?
" God wasteth naught.
Think you in vain
He sowed in thy childhood
Thought-seed in the brain,
And the joy to create,
Like his own joy, and will,
Like a fragment of fate
For the godlike control
Of the heaven of thy angels,

2

The loves of thy soul?
Ay, strong for the rule
Of devils that tempt thee,
Of demons that fool?
Shall so much of Him
Merely perish in haste,
Just stumble, and die,
And Death be a jester's mad riddle
Without a reply?
And Life naught but waste?
Behold, it is day,"
Saith the soul.
   1890.

MASTER FRANÇOIS VILLON,

AND OTHER POEMS.

MASTER FRANÇOIS VILLON.[1]

THE COUNT DE LILLE.

THE SEIGNEUR DE LUCE.

Time, circa 1463.

DE LUCE.

OUR good Duke Charles, you tell me, fain would know
Where bides this other rhymer.   Be it so.
I might have said, I know not : for to lie
Is easy, natural, and hath brevity
To win its hearing favour, whilst the truth
Spins out forever like a woman's youth,
And lacks the world for ally.   But mere pride
Would make me honest.   Let the duke decide
'Twixt boor and noble.   Ah ! 't was gay, I think,
When we were lads together.   What ! not drink ?
Then, by St. Bacchus, here 's to you, my lord !
Men say that luck, a liberal jade, has poured
Her favours on you : lordships half a score,
Castles and lands, that vineyard on the Loire ;
Something too much for one who lightly leaves
Such wine as this.   Alas ! who has, receives.

DE LILLE.

Come when you will and share it. I have served
God and the king. What fortune I 've deserved
The good saints know; through many a year I 've
    played
The games of war and peace. My father's blade
Has no stain on it. That, it seemeth me,
Were pleasant to the conscience, when set free
From war and council and grown old and gray
Fades in monastic peace one's life away.
These war-filled years gone by since last we met
Have had their griefs. What of yourself? Forget
My fates and me. I think the latter wars
Have missed your helping. As for me, my scars
Count half these years.

DE LUCE.

          Well, as chance willed, I fought
In Spain, or Italy, or France, and brought
Some pretty plunder back ; have killed my share,
Dutch, Don, or Switzer, any — everywhere
That bones were to be broken and the fare
And game were good ; have taken soldier pay
On this side and on that. In wine or play
Spent gayly ; found life but a merry friend
That lent, and then forgot the debt. To end,
Came home. And now my tale. On Easter day
It lost its hero.
          Silence, once 't is broke,

Can no man mend. 'T was thus this fellow spoke
Of whom I talk.   I never owned the thing
Folks like to label conscience, which the king
Packs wisely on his chancellor.   My device,
' *Suivez le Roi,*' suits well with life.   Not nice
Need one to be who Louis, or the rest,
Loyally follows, — taking what is best
Each good day offers ; yet, sometimes, De Lille,
Woman or wine, or one's too ready steel,
Lures one a trifle past the line of sport,
And then, — you see my point, — a friend at court
Perchance is needed.   Gossip, hereabout,
Which spreads like oil on water, leaves no doubt
That I should speak.   That wastrel had a way,
A trick of speech, as when he said, one day,
" The pot of Silence cracked, 't were best to break."
Strange how his words stay with me !   Half awake
Last night, I saw him, laughing too, and gay,
A grinning ghost, De Lille.   What priest could lay
A rhyming, jesting fiend ?   I have killed men,
Ay, and some pretty fellows too, but then
None troubled sleep.   This dead man, like an owl,
Roosts, wide-eyed, on my breast, — a feeble fowl —
Mere barnyard fowl at morn, — a carrion ghost.
The Devil has bad locks to keep his host
Of poets, thieves, and tipplers.

DE LILLE.

                    Think you so ?
No man can tell, De Luce, when some chance blow

Shall give him memories none may care to know.
Once, when we charged nigh Burgos, sorely pressed,
I drove my rapier through a youngster's breast
In wild fierce mellay when none think, — and yet
I see him, — see him reeling ; never can forget
His large eyes' sudden change, that one long cry !
'T was but a moment, and the charge went by.
Some unknown woman curses me in sleep,
Mother or mistress ; why does memory keep
These nettles, let the roses fall? Well ! well !
What more, De Luce ? The tale you have to tell
Is told a friend !

DE LUCE.

Three bitter years ago
A woman every year more fair, one Isabeau,
A Demoiselle De Meilleraye, began
To twist this coil which later cost a man
A pleasant reckless life, and you my tale.
Maids have I loved a many, widows frail
Loved *par amour*, but this one gayly spun
A pretty net about me.   It was done
Before I fully knew, and once begun
No fly more surely netted.   Ever still
The web is on me.   At her merry will
What pranks she played ! — and I a fettered slave
Was black or white, was all things blithe or grave
As met her humour.   Many a suitor came
Because her lands were broad, and, too, the game

Worth any candle. She but laughed. Some flared,
Or sputtered, and went out. My lady shared
Their woe but little. As for me, I fought
A good half dozen lordlings, also caught
A hurt or two. But then, ah ! that was worse,
A fellow came who wooed my dame in verse,
And did it neatly, — made her triolets
Rhyming her great blue eyes to violets ;
Wrote chansons, villanelles, and rondelettes,
Sonnets, and other stuff, and chansonnettes,
And jesting, rhymed the colour of my nose
With something, — possibly an o'erblown rose.
No need to say we fought, but luck went hard,
I thrust in tierce. He parried, broke my guard,
And then, I slipped, — St. Denis ! but I lay
A good six weeks to ponder on the way
The rascal did the thing. And he the while
Had to himself my lady's gracious smile ;
Whereon we played the game again, and time
Was that to which my rhymer ceased to rhyme.
A pretty trick there is, De Lille, you see
I learned in Padua ; this way, on one knee
To drop a sudden ; then a thrust in quarte
Settles the business. You shall learn the art.
'T is very simple. Ah ! before he died
He fumbled at his neck, and vainly tried
To snatch at something, till at last I took
A locket from him, for his own hand shook,
As well might be. He had but only breath

To mutter feebly " Isabeau," then death
Had him, and I the locket — have it still,
And some day she shall have it — in my will,
For scourge of memory.   This same Isabeau
Wept as a woman does, whilst to and fro
I wandered, waiting till the mood should go,
Then came again and found my lady fair
Reading my dead man's chansons.   Little care
Had she for others.   I, a love-fool, spent
The summer days like any boy, intent
To fit my will to hers.   I laugh again
To think I vexed my battle-wildered brain
In search of rhymes. — You smile, my lord ?   'T is so,
To find me gallant rhymes to Isabeau.
Pardie, De Lille, she rhymed it thrice to — No !
Swore none could love who lacked the joyous art
To love in song.
    Now, really when the heart
Gives out, and knows no more, one asks the head
To help that idiot ass.   Some one has said, —
Ah ! that man said it, — said, " 'T is heads that win
In love's chuck-penny game."   And I had been
The heart's fool quite too long. —
      At last, one day,
Hunting by St. Rileaux, I lost my way,
And wandering, lit upon a man who lay
Drowsing, or drunk, or dreaming mid the fern.
Quite motionless he stayed, as in I turn,
And say, " Get up there, villein ! Ho ! in there, —

Get up, and pilot me the way to Claire!"
On this rose lazily a lean, long man ;
Yawned, stretched himself, — with eyes as brown as tan,
And somewhat insolent, regarded me ; a nose
Fine as my lady's ; red, too, I suppose,
With sun, or just so much of sun as glows
Shut up in wine : and thus far not a word.
Till I, not over gay, or somewhat stirred
By this brute's careless fashions, wrathful said,
"Art dumb, thou dog?" But he untroubled laid
His elbow 'gainst a tree trunk, set his hand
To prop his head, and then, —
                            " I understand.
You lost the way to Claire, while I have lost
The gladdest thought that haply ever crossed
A poet's brain. Think what it is, fair sir,
To feel within your soul a gentle stir,
To see a vision forming as from mist,
And just then as your lips have almost kissed
This thing of heaven, to have a man insist
You show the way to Claire. A man may die
And still the world go on, but songs that fly
From laughing lip to lip, and make folk glad,
Have more than mortal life. 'T is passing sad.
You 've killed a thing had outlived you and me,
Bishops and kings, and danced a voice of glee
On lovers' tongues." Loudly I laughed and long.
"Mad! mad!" I cried; "the whole world 's mad in
    song.

Out-memory kings? What noble trade have you
That rate a king so low? Speak out, or rue
The hour we met. Your name, your name, man, too,
Unless you like sore bones." At this he stayed,
No more disturbed than I, and undismayed
Said, "François Villon de Montcorbier
Men call me ; but I really cannot say
I have not other names to suit at need,
As certain great folks have ; and sir, indeed
As to my trade, I am a spinner, and I spin,
As please my moods, gay songs of love or sin,
Sonnets or psalms — could make a verse on you.
Hast ever heard my ' Ballade des Pendus ' ?
I gave the verse a certain swing, you see,
That humours well the subject ; you 'll agree
To read it really shakes one ; many a thief
That verse has set a-praying. To be brief —
Ah, you 'll not hear it ? — then, sir, by my sword, —
But that 's in pawn, — or better, by my word, —
I can't pawn that, — ye saints ! if I but could !
Now just to pay your patience, — leave the wood
At yonder turning ; then the road to Claire
Lies to the left ; but you must be aware
The day is somewhat warm, and pray you try
To think how very, how unnatural dry
I am inside of me ; for outwardly,
Thanks to the dews, I 'm damp ; but could I put
My outside inside, — Ah ! your little but
Is really quite a philosophic thing

For lords who lose their way, and men who sing.
The simple fact is, I am deadly dry —
And that mere text once out, the sole reply,
The sermon, lies within your purse." I said,
" Had you not put a notion in my head,
I long ago had broken yours. Instead,
Sell me its use awhile." " If talk be dull,"
Cried he, " 'twixt one who fasts and one who 's full,
St. George ! 't is duller than the dullest worst
When one of them is just corpse-dry with thirst.
Once, by great Noah ! a certain bishop-beast
Kept me for three long summer months at least
On bread and water, — water ! Were wine rain
I never, never could catch up again."
Well, to be brief, De Lille, just there and then
We drove an honest bargain. He, his pen
Sold for so long as need was, — I, to get
Three times a week some joyful rondelette,
Sirventes satiric, competent to fit
The case of any wooing, versing wit,
Dizains, rondeaux, and haply pastourelles,
With any other rhyming devil-spells
A well-soaked brain might hatch, whilst I agreed
To house, clothe, wine the man, and feed.
That day we settled it at Claire. A tun
Of Burgundy it took before 't was done.
And then, to ease him at his task, you know,
Smiling he queried of this Isabeau :
Her eyes, her lips, her hair ; because, forsooth,

" The trap of lies were baited best with truth."
Quoth I, half vexed, " Brown-red, her hair."   " I
      know,"
My poet says ; " gold — darkened, like the glow
The sunset casts, to crown a brow of snow."
Then I, a love-sick fool ! — " She has a way —
Of " — " Yes, I understand ; as lilies sway
When south winds flatter, and the month is May,
And love words has the maiden rose to say."
Here pausing, suddenly he let his head
Rest on his hands, and, half in whisper, said,
" Alack !   Full many a year the daisies grow
Where rests at peace another Isabeau."
" The devil take thy memories ! Guard thy tongue ! "
Said I. What chanced was droll, for quick tears, wrung
From some low love-past, tumbled in his wine :
Cried he, " The saints weep through us.   Can these
      tears be mine ?
The dead are kings and rule us " — drank the liquor
      up,
Laughed outright like a girl, and turned the cup,
With " Never yet before, since life was young,
Did I put water in my wine," then flung
The glass behind him, shouted, " Quick, a bottle ! —
Another ; grief is but a thief to throttle.
Ho ! let the ancient hangman Time appear
And tuck it a neat tie beneath the ear.
      Many a trade has master Time.
      He sits in corners, and spinneth rhyme.

He is a partner of master Death,
Puffs man's candle out with a breath,
Leaves the wick to sputter and tell
In a sort of odorous epitaph
How foul the thought of a man may smell
For the world that lives, and has its laugh.
Ha! but Time has many trades!
Something in me now persuades
Master Time, grown debonair,
Hath turned for me a potter rare,
And made him a vase beyond compare:
Here below, a rounded waist,
Fit with roses to be laced ;
Rising, ripely curved above
Into flowing lines of love.
Thinking, too, how sweet 't would grow,
Time called the proud vase Isabeau."
" By every saint of rhyme," laughed I, " good fellow,
If this a man can do when rather mellow " —
"What shall he do ripe-drunk ? " he cried ; " erelong
The vine shall live again a flower of song."
How much he drank that six months who may know?
He kept his word.   There came a noble flow, —
Rondels and sonnets, songs, gay fabliaux,
Tencils, and virelais, and chants royaux,
That turned at last the head of Isabeau.
For, by and by, he spun a languid lay
Set her a weeping for an April day.
And then a reverdie, I scarcely knew

Just what it meant; by times the damsel grew
Pensive and tender, till at last she said, —
You see the bait was very nicely spread, —
" How chances it, fair sir, this gift of song
Lay thus perdu? You did yourself a wrong:
But now I love you, — love as one well may
A heart that hides its treasures, yet can say
At last their sweetness out. This simple lay! —
How could you know my thoughts?"
On this in haste
I cast an arm around her little waist,
And kissed her lips, and murmured tenderly
Some pretty lines my poet made for me,
And this occasion's chance.
So there, the dame
Well wooed and married, ends this pleasant game.

DE LILLE.

I knew your poet once, — of knaves the chief,
A gallows-mocking brawler, guzzler, thief, —
This orphan of the devil won with song
Our good Duke Charles, who thinks of no man wrong,
And least of all a poet. Once or twice
Duke Charles has saved his neck. One can't be nice
With poet friends, nor leave them in the lurch
Because they stab a man, or rob a church.
Also, that hog-priest-doctor, Rabelais,
Kept him a while, then bade the vagrant go
For half a nightingale and half a crow.

So there he slips from sight.   Then comes a tale
That stirs our rhyming Duke.   I must not fail
To know the sequel.

DE LUCE.

     Months went by.   My man
I had no need for ; soon my dame began
To droop and wilt, and, too, I knew not why,
To watch me sidewise with attentive eye,
Or stay for silent hours cloaked with thought,
Laughing or weeping readily at naught.
What changes women ?   A wife is just a wife.
The thing tormented me, for now her life
Faced from me ever, and, her head bent low,
She lived with some worn sonnet or rondeau
Had served its purpose.   Vexed at last, I took
The wretched stuff, the whole of it, and shook
The fragments to the winds.   Now, by St. George !
The thing stuck ever bitter in my gorge,
That such a peasant-slave's mere words should be
The one strong bond that held this love to me,
That was my life, and is.   Alas ! in vain
I played the lover over, till in pain
Because she pined, poor fool, I sought again
My butt of verse and wine, and gayly said,
" Here, fellow, there 's for drink !   Set me your head
To verse me something honest, that shall speak
A strong man's love, and to my lady's cheek
Fetch back its rose again."   But as for him,

This hound, he studied me with red eyes, dim
And dulled with wine, and lightly laughing cried,
" Not I, my lord.   Not ever, if I tried
The longest day of June.   Your falcon caught,
Be sure no jesses by another wrought
Will hold a captive ; " and with rambling talk
Put me aside, sang, hummed, took up the chalk
The landlord wont to score his drinks withal,
A moment paused, and scribbled on the wall,
      " If God love to a sexton gave,
         Surely he would dig it a grave ;
         If God fitted an ass with wings,
         What would he do with the pretty things ? "
I cursed him for a useless sot, but he,
Leering and heedless, scrawled unsteadily
Just " Wallow, wallow, wallow, this from me
To all wise pigs that on this mad earth be ; "
Wrote " François Villon " underneath, and there,
Smitten with drink, dropped on the nearest chair
And slept as sleep the dead.   I in despair
Went on my way.
                     But she, my gentle dame,
Grew slowly feebler, like an oilless flame,
Until this cursed thing happened.   On a day
I chanced upon her singing, joyous gay ;
Glad leapt my hopes.   I kissed her, saw her start,
Grow sudden pale, a quick hand on her heart. —
'Fore God I love her dearly, but I tore
A paper from her bosom, yet forbore

One darkened moment's time to read it, then
Saw the wild love verse, knew what drunken pen
Had dared. —
                    Fierce-eyed she stayed a little space,
Then struck me red with words, as if my face
A man had struck, saying, " What can be more base
Than bribe a peasant soul to win with thought
Above your thinking what you vainly sought?
I love you?   No — I loved the man who knew
To tell the gladness of his love through you ;
A thief, no doubt ; and pray what was he who
Thus stole my love?   You lied! and he, a sot!
A sot, you say, could rise above his pot, —
You never !   Love me !   Could one like you know
In love's sweet climate truth and honour grow? "
But I, seeing my folly clear, said, " Isabeau,
What matters it if I but used the flow
Of this man's fantasies to word the praise
I would have said a hundred eager ways
And moved you never?   Is it rare one pays
A man to sing? "
                    " Henceforth, my lord," said she,
" We talk tongues strange to each, but ever he
Talked that my heart knows best.   Your wife am I,
That 's past earth's mending ; what is left but try
To weary on to death?   What else? "   I turned,
Cried, " But I loved you well !   This boor has earned
A traitor's fate."
                    " And you," she moaned ; nor more,

Save, " Let *all* traitors die," and on the floor
Fell in a heap.   Thenceforward half distraught
I sought my poet thief, but never caught
The cunning fiend, till as it chanced one night,
My horse fallen lame, I, walking, saw the light
Still in her window. There below it stood
A man where fell the moonlight all aflood,
And suddenly a hand of mastery swept
The zittern, and — a whining love song leapt.
Ah ! but too well knew I the song he sang ;
I smiled to think it was his last. It rang
Mad chimes within my head. " Now then," I cried,
"A dog-life for a love-life ! " Quick aside
My poet cast his zittern, drew his sword,
Tried as he stood his footing on the sward,
And laughed. He ever laughed, and laughing said,
" Before we two cut throats, and one is dead,
And talk gets quite one-sided, let me speak,
Perchance it may be this rat's final squeak ;
Even a cat grants that, my lord, you know.
Speak certain words I must of this dame Isabeau.
An if you will not, this have I to say,
These legs of mine have ofttimes won the day,
And may again if I have not my way.
My thanks. You 're very good, and now, — what if
Full twenty dozen times a week a whiff
Of some sweet rose is given just to smell,
The rose unseen, — you catch my meaning ? — Well,

One haply gets rose-hungry, and erelong
Desires the rose. You think I did you wrong
Who bade me see her as one sees in song,
Her neck, her face, the sun-gloss of her hair,
Eyes such as poets dream, the love-curves fair;
These have you seen, but as for me, they were
Unseen of sense more lovely.
                                    Mark, my lord,
How sweet to-night the lilies. Pray afford
A moment yet to my life out of yours. Believe
A thing so strange you may not, nor conceive :
This woman, on the beauty of whose face
I never looked, nor shall, — whose virgin grace
I sold to you, — is mine while time endures.
Yea, for thy malady earth has no cures;
A brute, a thief am I that caged this love.
A sodden poet ! Some one from above
Looks on us both to-night ; you nobly born,
I in the sties of life. I do repent
In that I wronged this lady innocent.
But if you live or I, where'er she bide,
One François Villon walketh at her side.
Kiss her ! Your kiss ? It will be I who kiss.
Yea, every dream of love your life shall miss
I shall be dreaming ever !
                                    Well, the cat,
Patient or not, has waited. As for that
Be comforted. Hell never lacks reward
For them that serve it. Thanks. — On guard. On
        guard."

No word said I.   Long had I listened, dazed.
Now scorn broke out in hatred ; crazed,
Fiercely I lunged.   He laughing, scarce so rash,
Parried and touched my arm.   The rapier clash
Went wild a minute ; then a woman's cry
Broke from the hedge behind him, and near by
Some moonlit whiteness gleamed.   He turned, and I,
By heaven ! 't was none too soon, I drove my sword
Clean through the peasant dog from point to guard,
And held her as I watched him.   Better men
A many have I killed, but this man ! — Then
He staggered, reeling, clutched at empty air
And at his breast, and pitching here and there,
Fell, shuddered, and was dead.
                              By Mary's grace,
The woman kneeling kissed the dead dog's face !

Take you the Duke my tale.   The woman lives.
The man is dead.   None know but she.   What gives
Such needless haste to go ?   'T is not yet late.
Think you the story of this peasant's fate
Will vex Duke Charles ?   How looks the thing to
      you ?
No comment ?   None ?

DE LILLE.

                        None I could well afford
To speak.   The Duke must judge, not I.

DE LUCE.

My lord,
Your fashions like me not, and plainly, mine
Are somewhat franker.

DE LILLE.

I must ride.   The wine?

DE LUCE.

I pay for that.   The man who drinks must pay,
" The wine of friendship lasteth but a day,"
So said that pot-house Solomon.   I suppose
'T is easily thinned with time.   As this world goes,
A sorry vintage.
  1890.

HOW THE POET FOR AN HOUR WAS KING.

ONCE in a garden space, Saädi saith,
I came upon a tower, where within
There lay a king imprisoned until death
Should set him free ; and thinking deep of sin,
And those who took its madness to and fro
Below the dead hope of these prison bars,
I saw the thoughtless stream of pleasure flow
Till evening, and the sad reproachful stars
Loosed a great sorrow on me for this king
To whom in other days I joyed to sing.
Himself had trained himself to noble use
Of that great instrument, a man ; abuse
Of power he knew not ; never one
So served victorious virtue.   Then there came
Defeat and ruin.   Now no more the sun
Shall see again his face who reckoned fame
As but an accident of righteous deeds.
Thus evening found me thinking how exceeds
Man's strangest dream, what Allah wills for him,
Till through the shadows of the twilight dim

I heard the gray muezzin call to prayer.
Upon the sands I knelt alone, and there
Entreated Allah till the middle hour.
Among the palms that were around the tower
Came, as if pitiful, the nightingale,
And sang and sang as if 't were sin to fail ;
Whilst I who loved this great soul come to naught
Stayed wondering if any solace brought
The happy song that knows not pain of thought.
But then I heard above me, clear and strong,
The king's voice rising gather force of song,
Till from the prison wall its tameless power
Triumphant rang, as in some doubtful hour
Of angry battle, or when from defeat
It called again the shame of flying feet.
Now like a war drum rolling far away
Its stormy rhythms died.   No voice may say
Its after sweetness, for, as falls a bird
That high in air hath on a sudden heard
Its little ones below, and surely guessed
The lonely sadness of the yearning nest,
Fell earthward pitiful the singer's verse,
Cradled the many griefs of man, the curse
Of pain, of sin, and in its soothing rhyme
Rocked into peace these petty woes of time.
Till I, who would have given a caliph's gold
For consolation, was myself consoled.
Musing, I said, " Lo ! I will be this king,
Because a poet can be anything,

And may inhabit for a wilful hour
A maiden heart, or haunt a dewy flower,
Or be the murdered, or the murderer's hate."
I gathered up all knowledge, small or great,
Men had of him who sang, when his estate
Knew power and its danger.　How he ruled
A wayward race I knew ; how sternly schooled
His gentleness to give large justice sway ;
How helped the kindly arts of peace, and gay
And masterful of all that makes life sweet,
The jewel love set in this crown complete.
These, and much other garnered up from thought,
I took — and lo, how strange !　A moment brought
The whole to oneness, as when on a glass
The sun-rays fall, and bent together pass,
And glowing, flash a point of burning light ;
So, for a time I was the king that night.

A king was I, — a king of Allah's birth,
In one brief hour I lived long years of earth.
I broke the robber tribes who vexed with wrong
My peaceful folk.　Yea, as the simoon strong
That hurls the sands of death, in will and deed
A king I rode.　Then saw my regal state
Fall from me ruined, and a brutal fate
Wreck law and justice ; with a tranquil face
Beheld die out of life its joy and grace,
And quick death busy with whate'er I loved.
All these I saw, but with a heart unmoved,

And marvelled at myself, as in a dream
A man hath wonder when his visions seem
Fitting and true to sense. And so erelong,
Considering what fault had let the wrong
O'ercome the right, I lost myself in song.

Am I the potter? Am I the clay?
Allah, Thou knowest! Soft and gray
Fall the curling shreds away.
Lo, the noiseless feet of years
Swift the rhythmic treadle ply;
Hath the potter doubts and fears?
Is the clay kept soft with tears?
Still the busy wheel doth fly.
He is the potter, I am the clay;
Swiftly drop the ribands gray,
Flower and vine leaf silently grow,
Strong and gracious the vase doth show,
Firm and large, — the cup of a king.
Hither and thither wandering
The potter's fingers deftly smooth
Tangled tracery, and groove
Emblems, texts, the rose of love.
Suddenly his fingers slip,
Cracks the ever-thinning lip.
Was it the potter? Was it the clay?
Allah! Allah! who can say?
And the king I was that night
Smiled, to see the potter's plight.

I am the potter, I am the clay,
Spinning fall the earth-threads gray,
Deftly moulded, strong and tall
Grows the vase, and over all
Bud and roses, vine and grape,
Twine around its comely shape.
Was it potter?   Was it clay?
Did the potter's hand betray
Indecision?   Who can say?
At his feet the fragments roll ;
Lo, beside the wheel he stands
Wondering, with idle hands.
Let him gather up his soul
And make the clay a poor man's bowl !

Thus said the quiet king I was that night,
And o'er me grew the life of morning light,
While from the constant minaret above,
As drops a feather from the angel love,
Fell the first call to prayer, and overhead
A strong voice from the prison tower said,
" Allah il Allah ! God is ever great.
Time is his prophet for the souls who wait."
1890.

A PSALM OF THE WATERS.

Lo ! this is a psalm of the waters, —
The wavering, wandering waters :
With languages learned in the forest,
With secrets of earth's lonely caverns,
The mystical waters go by me
On errands of love and of beauty,
On embassies friendly and gentle,
With shimmer of brown and of silver.
In pools of dark quiet they ponder,
Where the birch, and the elm, and the maple
Are dreams in the soul of their stillness.
In eddying spirals they loiter,
For touch of the fern-plumes they linger,
Caress the red mesh of the pine roots,
And quench the strong thirst of the leafage
That high overhead with its shadows
Requites the soft touch of their giving
Like him whose supreme benediction
Made glad for love's service instinctive
The heart of the Syrian woman.
O company, stately and gracious,

That wait the sad axe on the hillside !
My kinsmen since far in the ages
We tossed, you and I, as dull atoms
The sport of the wind and the water.
We are as a greater has made us,
You less and I more ; yet forever
The less is the giver, and thankful,
The guest of your quivering shadows,
I welcome the counselling voices
That haunt the dim aisles of the forest.

Lo, this is a psalm of the waters
That wake in us yearnings prophetic,
That cry in the wilderness lonely
With meanings for none but the tender.
I hear in the rapids below me
Gay voices of little ones playing,
And echoes of boisterous laughter
From grim walls of resonant granite.
'T is gone — it is here — this wild music !
Untamed by the ages, as gladsome
As when, from the hands of their Maker,
In wild unrestraint the swift waters
Leapt forth to the bountiful making
Of brook and of river and ocean.
I linger, I wonder, I listen.
Alas ! is it I who interpret
The cry of the masterful north wind,
The hum of the rain in the hemlock,

As chorals of joy or of sadness,
To match the mere moods of my being?
Alas for the doubt and the wonder!
Alas for the strange incompleteness
That limits with boundaries solemn
The questioning soul! Yet forever
I know that these choristers ancient
Have touch of my heart; and alas, too,
That never was love in its fulness
Told all the great soul of its loving!
I know, too, the years, that remorseless
Have hurt me with sorrow, bring ever
More near for my help the quick healing,
The infinite comfort of nature;
For surely the childhood that enters
This heaven of wood and of water
Is won with gray hairs, in the nearing
That home ever open to childhood.

And you, you my brothers, who suffer
In serfdom of labour and sorrow,
What gain have your wounds, that forever
Man bridges with semblance of knowledge
The depths he can never illumine?
Or binds for his service the lightning,
Or prisons the steam of the waters?
What help has it brought to the weeper?
How lessened the toil of the weary?
Alas! since at evening, deserted,

4

Job sat in his desolate anguish,
The world has grown wise ; but the mourner
Still weeps and will weep ; and what helping
He hath from his God or his fellow
Eludes the grave sentinel reason,
Steals in at the heart's lowly portal,
And helps, but will never be questioned.
Yea, then, let us take what they give us,
And ask not to know why the murmur
Of winds in the pine-tree has power
To comfort the hurt of life's battle,
To help when our dearest are helpless.
Lo, here stands the mother.   She speaketh
As when at his tent door the Arab
Calls, Welcome ! in language we know not ;
Cries, Enter, and share with thy servant !
    1890.

COLERIDGE AT CHAMOUNY.

I WOULD I knew what ever happy stone
Of all these dateless records, gray and vast,
Keeps silent memory of that sunrise lone
When, lost to earth, the soul of Coleridge passed
From earthly time to one immortal hour :
There thought's faint stir woke echoes of the mind
That broke to thunder tones of mightier power
From depths and heights mysterious, undefined ;
As when the soft snows, drifting from the rock,
Rouse the wild clamour of the avalanche shock.

Who may not envy him that awful morn
When marvelling at his risen self he trod,
And thoughts intense as pain were fiercely born,
Till rose his soul in one great psalm to God.
A man to-morrow weak as are the worst,
A man to whom all depths, all heights belong,
Now with too bitter hours of weakness cursed,
Now winged with vigour, as a giant strong
To take our groping hearts with tender hand,
And set them surely where God's angels stand.

On peaks of lofty contemplation raised,
Such as shall never see earth's common son,
High as the snowy altar which he praised,
An hour's creative ecstasy he won.
Yet, in this frenzy of the lifted soul
Mocked him the nothingness of human speech,
When, through his being visions past control
Swept, strong as mountain streams. — Alas ! To reach
Words equal-winged as thought to none is given,
To none of earth to speak the tongue of heaven.

The eagle-flight of genius gladness hath,
And joy is ever with its victor swoop
Through sun and storm. Companionless its path
In earthly realms, and, when its pinions droop,
Faint memories only of the heavenly sun,
Dim records of ethereal space it brings
To show how haughty was the height it won,
To prove what freedom had its airy wings.
This is the curse of genius, that earth's night
Dims the proud glory of its heavenward flight.
1888.

DOMINIQUE DE GOURGUES.[2]

In his cheerful Norman orchard
Lay De Gourgues of Mont Marsan,
Gascon to the core, and merry,
Just a well-contented man,

With his pipe, that comrade constant,
Won in sorrowful Algiers,
In the slave's brief rest at evening
Left for curses and for tears.

Peacefully he pondered, gazing
Where his plough-ribbed cornfields lay,
With their touch of hopeful verdure,
Waiting patient for the May.

Joyous from the terrace o'er him
Came the voice of wife and child,
And the sunlit smoke curled upward
As the gaunt old trooper smiled.

" St. Denis," quoth the stout De Gourgues,
" Yon beehive's ever busy hum

Doth like me better than the noise
Of the musketoon and drum.

" Tough am I, though this skin of mine
By steel and bullet well is scarred,
Like those round pippins overhead
By the thrushes pecked and marred.

" Forsooth I 'm somewhat Autumn-ripe,
Yet like my apples sound and red.
And life is sweet," said stout De Gourgues,
" Yea, verily sweet," he said.

" Three things there were I once did love —
One that gay jester of Navarre,
And one to sack a Spanish town,
And one the wild wrath of war.

" And two there were I hated well
One that carrion beast a Moor,
And one that passeth him for spite,
That 's a Spaniard, rest you sure."

Still he smoked, and musing murmured,
" There be three things well I like,
My pipe, my ease, this quiet life,
Better far than push of pike.

" And to-day there be two I love
Who lured me out of the strife,

The lad who plays with my rusty blade,
And the little Gascon wife.

" Parbleu ! parbleu ! " cried gray De Gourgues,
For at his side there stood
A soldier, scarred and worn and white,
In a cuirass dark with blood.

" Ventre Saint Gris ! good friend, halloa !
Art sorely hurt, and how ? and why ?
Art Huguenot?   Here 's help at need,
Or Catholic ?   What care I ! "

No motion had the white wan lips,
The mail-clad chest no breathing stirred,
Though clear as rings a vengeful blade
Fell every whispered word.

" That Jean Ribaut am I
Who sailed for the land of flowers,
Fore God our tryst is surely set ;
I wearily count the hours."

And slowly rose the steel-clad hand,
And westward pointing stayed as set :
" Thy peace is gone !   No morn shall dawn
Will let thee e'er forget.

"Thy brothers, the dead, lie there,
Where only the winds complain,

And under their gallows walk
The mocking lords of Spain.

" They wait, these patient dead ;
They see, as dead men see,
The woman's endless tears,
The infant's careless glee.

" If ever this France be dear,
And honour as life to thee,
Wife and child are naught to-day,
Thy errand 's on the sea."

" St. Denis to save ! " cried stout De Gourgues,
" One may dream, it seems, by day."
The man was gone ! — but where he stood
A rusted steel glove lay.

" I 've heard — yea twice — this troublous tale,
It groweth full old indeed ;
But old or new my sword is sheathed
For ghost or king or creed."

Full slow he turned and climbed the hill,
And thrice looked back to see :
" The dream ! The glove ! — How came it there ? —
What matters a glove to me ? "

But day by day as one distraught
He stood, or gazed upon the board ;

Nor heard the voice of wife or boy,
Nor took of the wine they poured.

He saw his bannerol flutter forth,
As tossed by the wind of fight,
And watched his sword above the hearth
Leap flashing to the light.

He told her all. "Now God be praised!"
She cried, while the hot tears ran;
" She little loves who loves not more
His honour than the man."

His lands are sold. A stranger's hand
The juice of his grapes shall strain;
Another, too, shall reap the hopes
He sowed with the winter grain.

His way was o'er the windy seas,
But, sailed they fast or sailed they slow,
He saw by day, he saw by night,
The face of Jean Ribaut.

The sun rose crimson with the morn,
Or set at eve a ghastly red,
While over blue Bahama seas
Beckoned him ever the dead.

Till spoke, sore set at last, De Gourgues:
" Ho, brothers brave, and have ye sailed

For gain of gold this weary way ?
Heaven's grace ! but ye have failed !

" A sterner task our God hath set ;
In yon wild land of flowers
Our dead await the trusty blades
Shall cleanse their fame and ours.

" Ye know the tale."   Few words they said :
" We are thine for France to-day !"
By cape and beach and palmy isles
The avengers held their way.

The deed was done, the honour won,
Nor land nor gain of gold got they,
Where 'neath the broad palmetto leaves
Their dead at evening lay.

The deed was done, the honour won,
And o'er the gibbet-loads was set
This legend grim for priests to read,
And, if they could, forget.

" Not as to Spaniards : murderers these.
Ladrones, robbers, hanged I here,
Ransom base for the costly souls
Whom God and France hold dear."

How welcomed him that brave Rochelle,
With cannon thunder and clash of bell,

What bitter fate his courage won,
Some slender annals tell.

No legend tells what signal sweet
Looked gladness from a woman's eyes,
Or how she welcomed him who brought
Alas! one only prize, —

A noble deed in honour done
And the wreck of a ruined life.
Ah, well if I knew what said the lips
Of the little Gascon wife!
   1890.

THE WAVES AT MIDNIGHT.

THE CLIFFS, NEWPORT.

SEEN in the night by
Their snows, as they crush,
Evermore saying —
Hush — hush — hush —
They fall, and they die,
Break, and perish, without reply.

And are and are not,
And come back again
With the sob and throb
Of a constant pain,
And snatch from afar
The tremulous light of a single star.

Always the cliffs hear,
How mournfully sweet
Their murmurous music,
Their cry of defeat,
As near and more near
They shiver and die in darkness drear.

Bleaker the cliffs be,
And blacker the night,
Where tender with sorrow,
Where eager for light,
The waves of life's sea
Wail, crushed at an answerless cliff-wall for me.
  1889.

SEPTEMBER.

SIR GOLDENROD stands by and grieves
Where Queen September goeth by :
Her viewless feet disturb the leaves,
And with her south the thrushes fly,
Or loiter 'mid the rustling sheaves,
And search and fail, and wonder why.
The burgher cat-tails stiffly bow
Beside the marsh.   The asters cast
Their purple coronets, and below
The brown ferns shiver in the blast,
And all the fretted pool aglow
Repeats the cold, clear, yellow sky.
The dear, loved summer days are past,
And tranquil goes the Queen to die.
    1889.

BEAVER TAIL ROCKS.

CANONICUT.

FARE forth my soul, fare forth, and take thy own ;
The silver morning and the golden eve
Wait, as the virgins waited to receive
The bridegroom and the bride, with roses strown ;
Fare forth and lift her veil, — the bride is joy alone !
To thee the friendly hours with her shall bring
The changeless trust that bird and poet sing ;
Her dower to-day shall be the asters sown
On breezy uplands ; hers the vigour brought
Upon the north-wind's wing, and hers for thee
A stately heritage of land and sea,
And all that nature hath, and all the great have
    thought,
While low she whispers like a sea-born shell
Things that thy love may hear but never tell.
  1889.

OCTOBER.

STAY, gentle sunshine, stay ;
Sweet west wind bide awhile :
Nay, linger, and my maid
Shall bribe you with a smile.

Sweet sun and west wind stay,
You know not what you miss ;
Nay, linger, and my maid
Shall pay you with a kiss.
  1890.

YOU AND I.

WHAT would you say
If you were I,
And I were near,
And no one by ;
If you were I ?

What would you do
If you were I,
And night were dark,
And none were nigh ?
What would you do ?

What would I say
If I were you,
And none were near,
And love were true ?
What would I say ?

What would I do ?
Just only this.
And on my cheek

5

Soft lit a kiss.
This did she do!

I heard a cry,
And through the night
Saw far away
A gleam of white,
And there was I!

But not again
This she was I ;
Yet still I loved,
And years went by.
Ah, not again!
   1890.

TENNYSON.

THE larks of song that high o'erhead
Sung joyous in my boyhood's sky,
Save one, are with the silent dead,
Those larks that knew to soar so high.

But still with ever surer flight,
One laureate of unfailing trust
Chants at the gates of morn and night
Great songs that lift us from the dust,

And heavenward call tired hearts that grieve,
Beneath the vast horizon given
With larger breadth of morn and eve,
To this one lark alone in heaven.
    1890.

THE CARRY.

NIPIGON.

BLUE is the sky overhead,
Blue with the northland's pallor,
Never a cloud in sight,
Naught but the moon's gray sickle ;
And ever around me gray, —
Ashes, and rock, and lichen.
Far as the sick eye searches
Ghastly trunks, that were trees once,
Up to their bony branches
Carry the gray of ruin.
Lo ! where across the mountain
Swept the scythe of the wind-fall,
Moss of a century's making
Lies on this death-swath lonely,
Where in grim heaps the wood sachems,
Like to the strange dead of battle,
Stay, with their limbs ever rigid
Set in the doom-hour of anguish.
Far and away o'er this waste land
Wanders a trail through gray bowlders,
Brown to the distant horizon.
    1870.

OF A POET.

WRITTEN FOR A CHILD.

HE sang of brooks, and trees, and flowers,
Of mountain tarns, of wood-wild bowers,
The wisdom of the starry skies,
The mystery of childhood's eyes,
The violet's scent, the daisy's dress,
The timid breeze's shy caress.
Whilst England waged her fiery wars
He praised the silence of the stars,
And clear and sweet as upland rills
The gracious wisdom of her hills.
Save once when Clifford's fate he sang,
And bugle-like his lyric rang,
He prized the ways of lowly men,
And trod, with them, the moor and fen.
Fair Nature to this lover dear
Bent low to whisper or to hear
The secrets of her sky and earth,
In gentle Words of golden Worth.

1886.

NOTES.

[1] François Villon, born 1431, poet, thief, vagabond, led a life of excesses, in which were sharp experiences of prison and the torture-chamber. His ballad "Des Pendus" was written in 1461, whilst he was under sentence of death. Soon after he is lost to history, and becomes fair subject for the imagination. There is not the least foundation in any known facts for the story I have labelled with his name.

[2] In 1565, Menendez, an officer of Philip II. in Florida, put to death, under circumstances of strange atrocity, two hundred and eighty French Huguenots, most of whom were driven by starvation to surrender at discretion. Dominique de Gourgues, a French soldier, avenged this massacre as I have described, devoting to this purpose his fortune, and exposing himself to the malice of his own King, Charles IX. I have used a poet's license in the introduction of a supernatural influence. The tale is told at length by my friend Francis Parkman, in his "Pioneers of France in the New World."

.

www.ingramcontent.com/pod-product-compliance
Lightning Source LLC
Chambersburg PA
CBHW021522270326
41930CB00008B/1048